African

Grey Parrots

for Beginners

Basic Knowledge and Principles of Species-Appropriate Husbandry in the Domestic Aviary

ALINA DARIA

Contents

© *Jean van der Meulen*

Introduction

African grey parrots are a species within the parrot order ('Psittaciformes'). The scientific name of this particular species is 'Psittacus erithacus', where the first part of the species name - i.e., 'Psittacus' - stands for the genus.

African grey parrots belong to the family of so-called 'true parrots', which have the scientific name 'Psittacidae'. However, the family of cockatoos ('Cacatuidae'), which also belongs to the parrot order, is to be distinguished from this.

The species of African grey parrots, however, is nowadays still divided into two subspecies. The above scientific name 'Psittacus erithacus' is usually only used for the Congo African Grey Parrot. This name was first used in 1758 by the Swedish naturalist Carl von Linné (1707-1778).

The second subspecies of African Grey Parrot was only discovered a few decades later. It is the Timneh African Grey Parrot, which bears the scientific name 'Psittacus timneh'. It was given its name in 1844 by the British zoologist Louis Fraser (ca. 1820-1883).

A few more decades later, another subspecies of the African Grey Parrot was established by the British researcher Boyd Alexander (1873-1910). Boyd had discovered parrot specimens that were both darker and larger than the already established African Grey Parrots. Boyd Alexander named this new subspecies 'Psittacus princeps'. However, it is considered highly controversial whether the differences are actually so great that a new subspecies can be derived from them. This is often rejected in research. Therefore, usually only the two clear subspecies of Congo African Grey Parrot and Timneh African Grey Parrot are commonly used.

African Grey Parrots are considered to be extremely linguistically gifted and intelligent. As a result, they have become extremely popular pets, enhancing and enriching the lives of adults and children alike. Although they are only found in the wild in Africa, African Grey Parrots can be found as pets in many different countries and on all continents.

Unfortunately, the International Union for Conservation of Nature (IUCN) has classified African Grey Parrots as an endangered species since 2016. However, African Grey Parrots have been specially protected since 1981, as they fall under the so-called CITES (Washington Convention on International Trade in Endangered Species).

Six years later, special protection for African Grey Parrots was also declared in European law. In 2017, this protection was further tightened in the EU, as African Grey Parrots were included in Appendix A of the EU Species Protection Regulation that year.

Appendix A of this regulation lists particularly endangered species, which today unfortunately includes the African Grey Parrot. As a result of the listing, African Grey Parrots now have the highest protection status in the EU. This is due to excessive trapping and trade, as a result of which wild populations are declining.

Unfortunately, in order to meet the demand for African Grey Parrots in the international bird trade, African Grey Parrots are caught far too often, so that wild populations can no longer regulate themselves naturally. Another reason why African Grey Parrots are now considered an endangered species is that they are losing more and more of their habitat.

© *Muhammad Murtaza Ghani*

The Congo African Grey Parrot

When Carl von Linné described the Congo African Grey Parrot in 1758, he gave Gabon as its origin. Although this is correct and the Congo African Grey Parrot can still be found in Gabon today, its range extends to several other countries.

The Congo African Grey Parrot is not only native to Gabon, but also to Cameroon, Nigeria, Tanzania, Kenya, Ghana, Côte d'Ivoire and, of course, Congo. These are countries in West Africa and Central Africa. There it lives mainly in tropical rainforests and partly also in mangroves and wet savannahs. Mangroves are coastal forests. The roots of the trees and shrubs in these forests protrude from the water and have specially adapted to life so close to the water.

In the wild, Congo African Grey Parrots do not live alone, but in flocks. While during the day they move around either in pairs or in smaller groups, in the evening they gather in a usually very large flock to spend the night together.

Congo African Grey parrots live to be quite a bit older than "classic" pets, so be aware that a Congo African Grey parrot is a companion for life or a large part of life. It lives on average between 40 and 50 years. However, many specimens have been known to live well over 60 years!

When fully grown, the Congo African Grey Parrot reaches an average size of 30 to 40 centimetres (12 to 16 inches). The wingspan is between 46 and 52 centimetres (18 to 21 inches).

Congo African Grey Parrots weigh between 400 and 500 grams on average (between 0.9 and 1.1 pounds / between 14 and 18 ounces).

Their beak is completely black, and the head is much lighter than the body. While the body is grey, the head is predominantly white, especially around the eyes. In addition, the head is not feathered. But also overall the Congo African Grey Parrot is distinctly lighter than the Timneh African Grey Parrot. The upper half of the body is rather dark grey. This extends from the back to the wings, over the chest and also the upper belly. However, light grey undulations can also be found in these areas. The lower part of the body is lighter than the upper part, although not whitish as on the head, but rather light grey. This light grey area extends from the underbelly over the flanks to the tail, which is rather short for a parrot. The rectrices of the rounded control are about the same length. The rudder, upper and lower tail coverts are bright red - this is very striking and typical for this parrot.

But what are rectrices or what is the control at all? Rectrices are the tail feathers of the parrot. How long or short the rectrices are varies from species to species and depends, for example, on the way the bird flies.

With the help of the rectrices on the tail, birds can maintain their balance, control and adjust the directions of their flight and much more.

The iris of the Congo African Grey Parrot's eye is bright yellow, the claws are black (like the beak), and the toes have a light grey colouring.

Congo African Grey Parrots are - like all parrots - very social animals. They are no loners and have at least one companion.

If you keep parrots as pets, the natural living conditions should be recreated as well as possible - this applies to all species. Therefore, I recommend giving the parrot a mate because in the wild it is very likely to form a lifelong partnership. However, there are many countries in which it is normal to have a parrot in single housing. The pair is also a team when mating - while the female lays the eggs in tree cavities and incubates them there for about a month, the male watches over the female and her clutch, protects it and brings in food. When the young have hatched, both female and male take care of the offspring. The family stays together for a long time.

In the wild, Congo African Grey Parrots have some enemies - these include "ground walkers" as well as other birds. Especially cats of prey and birds of prey can make life difficult for the parrot. However, snakes, monkeys or other animals sometimes steal the eggs from the nest. If you keep parrots as pets, these risks are of course excluded - and if you also keep cats, for example, they should of course be kept well away from the parrots.

Furthermore, it is important to note that wild Congo African Grey parrots visit so-called clay licks several times a year. These are certain places on steep riverbanks where clay seeps out. At these places, the animals can absorb minerals through the clay, which help the body to detoxify - after all, healing clay (or healing earth) for humans is also known to detoxify the human body and remove harmful substances. If a Congo African Grey parrot does not live in the wild, it naturally cannot visit clay licks. Therefore, special attention must be paid to the balanced mineral budget.

The Timneh African Grey Parrot

The Timneh African Grey Parrot is often called "the little brother" of the Congo African Grey Parrot. It too is extremely popular but is less common as a pet worldwide than its big brother. While the Congo African Grey parrot is slimmer, more elongated and thus more graceful, the Timneh African Grey parrot is rather smaller and appears "stocky".

The Timneh African Grey Parrot grows to an average size of about thirty centimetres (twelve inches) and is thus literally the smaller brother of the Congo African Grey Parrot. The average weight of a Timneh African Grey Parrot is about 350 grams (roughly 12 ounces / 0.8 pounds).

The Timneh African Grey Parrot is not only smaller, but also darker overall. White areas are only found around the eye and possibly in places on the underbelly, although this is light grey rather than white overall. The upper half of the Timneh African Grey Parrot's body is also darker than the lower half. The rectrices in particular can almost fade into black. The neck and throat are covered with dark grey feathers, becoming lighter towards the underbelly.

The tail feathers are also red, but not as bright as the Congo African Grey Parrot's, but rather dark red or almost brownish and quite inconspicuous. The lower beak of the Timneh African Grey Parrot is also black, like that of the Congo African Grey Parrot, but the upper beak is lighter and more pink/beige.

The Timneh African Grey Parrot also lives mainly in humid areas, savannah forests and mangroves, but its range is smaller than the range of the Congo African Grey Parrot. This species lives primarily in Sierra Leone, Liberia, southern Guinea and the Republic of Côte d'Ivoire. All these countries are located on the coast of West Africa.

The Timneh is also a tree dweller, it is a cavity nester and nests in tree cavities. This is called "arbicol" (living in trees). The Timneh African Grey Parrot is unfortunately also an endangered species. The reasons for this are the same as for the endangerment of the Congo African Grey Parrot: on the one hand, the sometimes excessive capture and trade threatens the wild populations and, on the other hand, the species is also threatened by the destruction of its habitats.

The extent to which the two species differ in character is highly controversial. Character and behavioural differences cannot be clearly determined, as many keepers and breeders report different observations. Some people do not notice any other difference between the two species apart from the visual differences. Some report that the Timneh African Grey parrot is cheekier and more hyper than the Congo African Grey parrot. Other breeders report that the Timneh African Grey Parrot is shyer and timider than the Congo African Grey Parrot.

Presumably, this is simply a question of individual character. Each animal has its own personality. Overall, the Timneh African Grey Parrot is considered to be somewhat more difficult to tame than the Congo African Grey Parrot, but this can also differ from animal to animal due to the different characters and is not scientifically proven.

Single Keeping, Groups, Socialisation?

African grey parrots are social animals and live in a flock in nature. Almost all grey parrots have a permanent partner of the opposite gender, with whom they usually spend their entire lives. It is therefore very controversial whether grey parrots may be kept alone or not. This varies from country to country. In some countries there are even laws that stipulate that a grey parrot must not live alone. In other countries these laws do not exist.

You will probably hear different kinds of advice. My personal advice is not to keep a grey parrot in solitary confinement. Many people like to have a hand-raised parrot that lives alone so that it is particularly tame and very affectionate towards humans. It is understandable to want to have a very close bond with a pet. But it is better for the bird to have a partner as well. Parrots can still become tame and like humans, even if they have a parrot friend. But it is healthier for the parrot if it is allowed to live as it would in the wild - with a companion of the opposite gender.

If you keep a grey parrot alone, you must be aware that you will have to spend a lot of time with it. The grey parrot definitely needs some sort of partner and if it doesn't have another parrot as a partner, then it will look to a human as a partner. Therefore, the human needs to spend a lot of time with the bird, otherwise the bird will get lonely.

It is also important to know that the grey parrot may then become jealous of other humans, because it will see you as its mate and probably not like it when others get your attention.

It must also be said that of course it always depends on the individual case. First of all, there is the question of whether two grey parrots have a good relationship with each other at all, because in nature they can choose their own partner. If they are simply put together, they have not chosen their partner, but humans have. It is possible that the birds do not get along so well if they do not match in character.

Or there might be the case that one partner dies and the other lives on. Whether this parrot will then accept a new partner is also questionable. As you can see, there are many special cases and attention must always be paid to the individual character of the parrot.

Keeping African Grey parrots alone can in some cases lead to severe psychological and physical damage. In the wild, no African Grey parrot lives alone, but always in a more or less large flock. Of course, an African Grey Parrot can also be alone from time to time, for example when a male is looking for food for his breeding female. But after a short time, African Grey parrots always find their way back together. Most African Grey parrots form lifelong partnerships. Therefore, it is best to keep one female and one male together. If you want to keep more than two parrots, this is not a problem - ideally you should then add another pair, so that you have a total of two females and two males, each forming a pair. If you really have a lot of space and would like to increase the flock even more, you should also pay attention to a balanced ratio of males and females. The respective pairs do not have to be kept in separate aviaries, but can and should live together, because even in nature, an African Grey Parrot usually has a fixed partner, but often lives with this partner in a larger group.

A social animal that is deprived of companions of the same species naturally tries to compensate for this by "clinging" to the only living creature it has contact with - humans. So, if you have a single grey parrot, you will need to spend a great many hours a day with the animal so that it does not become lonely.

A hand-raised parrot that is kept alone needs constant and intensive occupation and entertainment by humans to avoid behavioural problems. Lonely parrots sometimes develop extreme behavioural disorders, suffer from depression and start plucking, for example. This means that they pluck out their own feathers because they suffer psychologically. A beginner is advised to only take in parrots in which no behavioural disorders are present.

Furthermore, it is not advisable to socialise African Grey Parrots with other bird species. Not all birds are the same and not all parrots are the same. Sometimes a Congo African Grey parrot is socialised with a Timneh African Grey parrot. This can work but it does not have to. There are usually no arguments for this either. In the wild, a Congo African Grey parrot will not choose a Timneh African Grey parrot as a mate, and a Timneh would not choose a Congo either. It is better and easier for all parties to stay with the same subspecies.

The claim that only parrots kept singly become tame is not correct. Couples also become tame when they are used to humans. Even whole flocks can get used to humans, become tame and often learn tricks.

African grey parrots are usually very open-minded, curious and sociable birds that usually get used to humans as "roommates" very well. Because of their intelligence, many parrots also enjoy being challenged and encouraged, for example by learning tricks. However, it is important that nothing is forced on the bird and that training is always done with mutual consent!

© *Muhammad Murtaza Ghani*

Purchasing African Grey Parrots

So, once you have decided to offer African Grey parrots a nice new home, the question naturally arises as to where the animals can be obtained from and what requirements need to be met. This varies greatly from country to country. This book is available in many countries all over the world, therefore, you should get familiar with the respective regulations in your country of residence.

For example, African grey parrots are particularly protected in the European Union (EU). Since 2017, African Grey parrots may only be bought and sold in the EU with a so-called EC trading certificate. This change came into force because it was decided at the 17th Conference on International Trade in Endangered Species of Wild Fauna and Flora that

African Grey Parrots should be listed in Appendix I of the Washington Convention on International Trade in Endangered Species of Wild Fauna and Flora (abbreviated to 'CITES') from this date onwards and thus receive the highest protection status that animals enjoy.

Both Timneh African Grey Parrots and Congo African Grey Parrots are affected. In most cases, this certificate is applied for by the seller or breeder. The application is usually made to the nature conservation authority. The certificate is mandatory in the EU, otherwise both seller and buyer are liable to prosecution.

Animals that were already kept before 2017 now also require an EC certificate if they are to be handed over to a different person. Without the certificate, an African grey parrot may not change ownership. If this does happen, it is a criminal offence by both parties.

For example, even if no sale is planned, it is important that every African Grey Parrot in Germany is registered with the nature conservation authority! It is the keeper's responsibility to comply with the obligation to register.

In Great Britain, for example, this is somewhat different. Here, too, a certificate is required for the purchase/sale, but if no change of ownership is planned at all, the African Grey Parrot does not have to be registered.

This is stated in a statement by the APHA ('The Animal and Plant Health Agency') ("No CITES licence will be required to keep an African Grey Parrot as a pet and they will not be required to be registered").

Nevertheless, documents should be available that can certify when and where the African Grey Parrot was acquired and where it originally came from.

However, it should also be noted that a certificate is not only required at the time of purchase, but also if the African Grey Parrot is to be transferred to another country.

In the United States of America, commercial cross-border trade in wild African Grey Parrots has been banned for a number of years, as it is in the other countries that adhere to CITES requirements. But they may still be bred and kept privately.

However, breeders must be registered with the Convention on International Trade in Endangered Species of Wild Fauna and Flora ('CITES' - see above). This is handled quite strictly in many countries to ensure that only reputable breeders appear on the market.

Furthermore, it should be possible to prove where the respective African Grey Parrot originates from - because unfortunately wild African Grey Parrots are still taken into captivity and traded today, mostly by smugglers and poachers. Stricter legislation and tracking will better protect African Grey Parrots. Therefore, it is normal for a parrot to come with "papers".

© *Zoosnow*

Furthermore, in some countries it is forbidden to keep African Grey parrots in solitary confinement. For example, in Switzerland, the Animal Welfare Act stipulates that African Grey parrots must be kept at least in pairs because they are social animals (Article 13 of the Animal Welfare Ordinance in conjunction with Appendix 2, Table 2). If an African Grey parrot is kept alone in Switzerland, a fine may be imposed and in the worst case the animal may be confiscated. However, these regulations do not exist in all countries - in some countries single keeping is prohibited, in others it is allowed.

Also, in Switzerland, for example, a certificate of competence is required if you want to keep large parrots - large macaws and cockatoos. There you need special knowledge and a licence not only for breeding, but also for purely private keeping. However, there are no restrictions for the private keeping of African Grey Parrots in this country.

Therefore, it is always important to familiarise oneself in advance with the respective regulations that apply in the country in which one lives. Once you have familiarised yourself with the applicable law, it is important to have your new additions thoroughly checked. This is especially important if a new animal is to be integrated into an existing group.

But even if it is a first-time acquisition, it is advisable to have the animal examined and/or to observe quarantine, as some diseases can also be passed on to humans and/or possible other pets. Some diseases can even be transmitted via feather dust. If the animal is examined by a doctor, it is advisable to have it tested at least for psittacosis (Chlamydia psittaci), avian bornavirus (PDD), polyomavirus, psittacine herpesvirus and PBFD (parrot beak and feather disease). We will look at these diseases in more detail later in the chapter "Ten common diseases".

Now there are several ways to acquire African Grey Parrots. Most people want to have young animals to watch the animal grow up and to spend as much time as possible with the animal. However, one should keep in mind that there are already a lot of (older) animals waiting for a beautiful new home. They were no longer wanted by their old owners or ended up in a rescue centre or animal shelter for other reasons.

Of course, it is possible that these animals have had bad experiences in the past and may be behaviourally disturbed. These animals are not recommended for a beginner and should be cared for by more experienced people. It is best to get advice on the spot and also to openly communicate that you have had no (or little) experience with parrots in the field. It is also a good idea to visit the animals in advance. You should also make sure that the animals look healthy and are well kept. The cloaca should not be dirty, and the plumage should not be plucked or dull.

Furthermore, the origin of the respective animals should be explained. There are usually documents for each parrot, at least the proof of origin is indispensable. It is perfectly normal that at least a protection fee is charged for the acquisition or adoption. This ensures that the new pet owners are serious about getting pets and the costs are covered. Reputable breeders and, of course, animal shelters and rescue centres take great care to ensure that their animals are placed in loving hands. Therefore, they will gladly advise newcomers and inform them about important aspects.

© Strichpunkt

The Home

Parrots need a lot of space! This will hopefully not surprise anyone. When keeping animals, one should already think carefully before acquisition or adoption whether one can offer the animal(s) relatively species-appropriate conditions. Parrots are among the pets that need the most space. If you do not have this space, it is better to choose another species of animal or at least another type of bird.

The parrot's enclosure is called an "aviary". An aviary is a particularly large cage in which it is possible for the birds to fly!

The aviary for a pair of African Grey parrots should have the minimum dimensions of 2 m x 1 m x 2 m (6.5 feet x 3 feet x 6.5 feet). It should therefore be at least two metres long, at least one metre wide and at least two metres high. If another pair is kept in the same aviary, the floor space (i.e., length x width) should be increased by at least half.

This also corresponds to the recommendation of the Veterinary Association for Animal Protection ('Tierärztliche Vereinigung für Tierschutz e. V.', Germany).

These dimensions are not recommended in all countries. In some countries there are legal regulations about how much space parrots must have, in other countries there are no laws.

When there are no laws, measurements are recommended inconsistently, and recommendations sometimes vary widely. For example, in the USA and UK, lower minimum measurements are recommended than in Germany or Switzerland.

However, one should be aware of one thing: In the wild, grey parrots have limitless space and can fly at any time, as much and as often and as far as they want. They move around a lot in nature and sometimes cover several miles a day. Therefore, one should put oneself in the grey parrot's place and ask oneself how we would feel if we were sitting in a small cage for many hours a day.

For those reasons, one should consider how much space one has at home and offer an aviary that is as large as possible. In the German expert opinion on the welfare of birds, especially on the minimum requirements for keeping parrots, only the dimensions 2 m x 1 m x 1 m (6.5 feet x 3 feet x 3 feet) are mentioned as minimum dimensions for parrots that reach a size between 25 and 40 centimetres (10 to 16 inches) - but this expert opinion dates back to 10 January 1995 and today there is a great deal of agreement in the parrot community that African Grey parrots need an aviary height of two metres.

Considering that African Grey parrots have many hectares of woodland available to them in the wild, the above measurements should be the minimum. It is important to emphasise again that the above parameters are only minimum dimensions. A larger aviary, or even a whole parrot room, is of course even better. The more space, the more comfortable the birds will feel!

Care should also be taken to ensure an appropriate temperature. As African Grey parrots originate from Africa, they do not cope well with cold temperatures. The temperature should therefore never drop below 15°C (60°F) - this is the absolute pain threshold. It is better if it is a little warmer. Room temperature (20°C / 70°F) is fine, in summer it can be warmer.

Furthermore, African Grey parrots should not spend the entire day in their aviary but should also be allowed to fly freely in the house ("free flight"). Of course, care should be taken that the parrots cannot escape through windows and doors - for their own good. This free flight should also be possible for several hours a day, not just one or two. If you don't want the parrots to move around the entire house, or if there are too many risks that the parrots could unintentionally fly outdoors, it is better to set up a whole parrot room or at least an extra-large aviary. If free flight is not possible often or for long, the parrots should live permanently in at least five square metres. Of course, it is best if the parrots have a whole room at their disposal!

The above conditions apply to indoor keeping. It is also possible to keep the animals outdoors, however, it should be noted that African Grey Parrots have their home in West and/or Central Africa and that warm temperatures prevail there accordingly. If you want to keep African Grey parrots outdoors, the animals need a shelter in addition to the outdoor enclosure, in which it must always be nice and warm - even in winter. The shelter should be as large as the minimum requirements for an indoor aviary (i.e., at least two square metres of floor space at a height of two metres).

The temperature in the shelter must always be above 15°C (60°F) so that the parrots can never get too cold. Room temperatures are better, around 20°C (70°F). The outdoor enclosure itself can be as big as you like. The more space the birds have, the happier they will be. However, to ensure that the parrots like to fly a lot, the outdoor enclosure should be at least five metres long.

© *Capri 23*

But no matter whether you keep African Grey parrots indoors or outdoors: The home must be varied and comfortably furnished.

So, what is the minimum equipment for a beautiful African Grey parrot home?

✓ at least four perches, also branches or twigs, preferably native deciduous trees

✓ lighting for bird housing systems (UV light for vitamin D3 formation and for UV-sensitive eyesight)

✓ destructible material (African grey parrots love to gnaw)

✓ nibbling possibilities

✓ climbing possibilities

✓ a bathing possibility for plumage care

✓ feeding place (daily cleaning and offer of fresh food)

✓ **drinking place (daily cleaning and offer of fresh drinking water)**

✓ **species-appropriate humidity, possibly with the help of a humidifier (air humidity at least 60%)**

Since parrots also like to gnaw on the grille of the aviary, this grille should not be galvanised or covered with plastic. Furthermore, care should be taken that the lamps do not flicker, as parrots perceive the lighting from conventional fluorescent tubes (without electronic ballasts) as flickering. This is called the "stroboscopic effect".

The UV lamps for birds should then shine between ten and fourteen hours a day if the parrots do not otherwise experience the natural day-night times, for example because there is not enough light coming through the window of the parrot's room. The parrots should be able to develop a natural day-night rhythm; therefore, the morning and evening twilight phases are also important.

Bathing in the aviary is very popular, as the parrots can groom and clean their feathers here. However, many parrots also like to be sprayed with water from spray bottles. Of course, parrots also defecate. How often the droppings should be removed depends on the size of the enclosure, the stocking and the time of year. On hot summer days, it is recommended to remove the droppings daily to keep flies away. Otherwise, in large enclosures it may be sufficient to remove the droppings only every few days.

© *Wasi 1370*

Diet and Nutrition

Animals are roughly divided into carnivores (meat eaters), herbivores (plant eaters), frugivores (fruit eaters) and omnivores ("everything eaters"). These head categories are often further subdivided into subcategories; for example, insectivores belong to the carnivores - and leaf-eaters belong to the herbivores.

African Grey Parrots are omnivorous animals. They feed on both animal and plant foods, but the vast majority of African Grey parrot food is plant-based and only a very small proportion is animal protein. In domesticated animals, the natural diet should be replicated as closely as possible. However, the (domestic) animal naturally does not have the opportunity to obtain and select its own food as it would in the wild. A domesticated animal can only eat the food that humans have previously selected for it. Therefore, it is the human's responsibility to choose the right food, offer the right amount and pay attention to the essential macronutrients and micronutrients.

First, let's look at what African Grey Parrots usually eat in the wild. There are of course regional differences, as African Grey Parrots are native to many countries in West Africa as well as Central Africa. This covers an extremely large area, in which there are of course also some differences. Nevertheless, it is easy to determine what African Grey Parrots mainly eat: fruit, nuts, berries, buds, flowers and seeds. However, parrots also often eat the plant parts themselves. Papaya, tamarind, the oil palm, millet, banana plants and maize plants, for example, belong to the main foods.

Exactly which plant foods an African Grey Parrot will eat depends, of course, on the season and the respective area. However, the African Grey Parrot has it comparatively easy here: it is a so-called 'generalist'.

In the animal world, a distinction is made between generalists and specialists. Generalist species can adapt quite well to their environment and use different resources, while specialist species use rather limited food resources and are therefore more dependent on their environment and the environmental conditions. Generalist species such as parrots can use a wide range of food resources and are not particularly choosy. They can therefore adapt well to their particular environment and living conditions.

In addition, as already explained, African Grey parrots regularly visit so-called clay licks in order to cover their need for essential minerals. Clay licks can be compared to the healing clay (or healing earth) that many people often consume to detoxify the body. Domesticated African grey parrots, of course, do not have access to this, so here too humans must ensure an adequate supply of the micronutrients.

Animal proteins play a minor role in the diet of the African Grey Parrot but should also be fed from time to time. The type of animal protein fed varies greatly from country to country and from breeder to breeder.

It is important to mention that birds do not tolerate dairy products well and do not need them. Birds do not drink milk as young animals (like mammals), nor do they require milk from another species as adults. Furthermore, milk can cause digestive problems in birds. There are parrot keepers who occasionally offer their birds, for example, low-fat curd cheese, but this is not necessary and offers no added value for the bird.

Sometimes African grey parrots are also offered the meat of cows or chickens. Again, this is not necessary. Feeding recommendations sometimes vary greatly, especially between different countries, but I always recommend following the natural diet in the wild. In the wild, an African Grey parrot does not eat meat from cows, chickens or similar, so it does not need to be fed to domesticated African Grey parrots.

In the wild, African Grey Parrots meet their animal protein requirements by eating insects and worms, for example. Snails are also on their menu from time to time. It is therefore a good idea to cover their animal protein requirements with these sources.

Particularly well suited are ...

... mealworms and maggots

(attention, high calories)

... brown shrimps

... caterpillars, waxworms

... termites

Other insects such as crickets, grasshoppers or cockroaches can theoretically also be eaten, but it has not been proven that African Grey Parrots feed on these insects in the wild. It is rather unlikely because these insects are rather difficult for the African Grey Parrot to catch in live form.

It is easier for it to catch caterpillars and the like.

In addition, a boiled egg may also be used as a source of animal protein.

However, animal food sources do not need to be offered often, as they only make up a very small part of the African Grey Parrot's diet. It is sufficient to offer an African Grey parrot an egg or some insects/worm every fortnight. Some keepers even offer this only once a month, others once a week. However, animal protein should not be fed more than once a week, as this would be too much. Too much animal protein can affect digestion as well as organ health, such as healthy kidney function.

To maintain a healthy kidney function, prevent dehydration and keep the rest of the organs in good health, fresh drinking water is of course essential - this applies to humans as well as African Grey parrots. Of course, African Grey parrots also consume water through fresh food, but fresh drinking water must be freely available to them in sufficient quantities around the clock. There should be at least one drinking place. The water should be changed daily, some keepers change it twice a day. In any case, the drinking place should be placed in such a way that they do not defecate into it.

© *Vieleineinerhuelle*

So, let's move on to the main food for African Grey parrots - the plant food. African Grey parrots need a healthy grain food on the one hand and fresh fruit and vegetables on the other, as well as possibly a few forage plants. The dry food, i.e., the grain food, should only contain a few nuts, if any, as nuts are healthy but also very high in fat and calories. Fat-rich seeds such as sunflower seeds are also healthy, but only in moderation, as they also contain many calories.

The diet of African Grey parrots should therefore be based on healthy grain food mixes (with healthy seeds), fruits, vegetables and herbs.

It is important to ensure that the grain mixes do not contain any unhealthy additives. These include, for example, salt and sugar, also in the form of molasses, vegetable and animal by-products and the like. If these ingredients appear in the ingredients list, it is a sign that great importance has been attached to the production of a cheap food. In the best case, the dry food should only contain natural wholefoods.

The same applies if you like to offer pellets. If in doubt, you can mix the dry food yourself by first buying the individual ingredients separately and then mixing them together. This also gives you more control over which ingredient goes into the food and how much, and that there are no unhealthy additives. A list of healthy grains/seeds is added at the end of this chapter.

Fruits, vegetables and herbs are the be-all and end-all of a healthy diet, as they provide plenty of fluids and many valuable vitamins. Fruit, vegetables and herbs should therefore be offered daily, preferably in thirds, so that not only highly sugary fruit, for example, is available, but also healthy herbs with bitter substances and the like.

In addition, make sure that different varieties are offered every day. Each food has a different nutrient composition and sometimes provides different vitamins, so it is important to ensure a varied diet.

Of course, it is not necessary to offer a new food every day and you should also pay attention to what the African Grey parrots find particularly tasty and prefer to eat. Nevertheless, the diet must of course be varied and diverse - just as with humans. Branches and leaves (especially from deciduous trees) are also very popular! However, special care must be taken to ensure that the tree species are not poisonous to parrots.

At the end of this chapter, you will find further lists of suitable fruits, vegetables and herbs.

One of the staple foods of wild African Grey parrots should not go unmentioned and be looked at a little more closely: Palm fruits! These are also called palm nuts and are one of the main food sources for many African Grey Parrots living in the wild. These fruits contain a lot of beta-carotene (➔ vitamins A, E) and thus contribute to overall health, especially strong immune system and eye health.

However, it is also true that palm fruit tends to be one of the higher fat foods. This is not a problem for free-ranging African Grey parrots as they get a lot of exercise during the day. Domesticated African Grey parrots move much less than wild animals.

If you want to feed palm fruit, you should pay close attention to its origin. Surely most people have already heard that palm oil is very harmful to the environment and is boycotted by many people. In fact, large areas of forest are cleared or deliberately set on fire in order to be able to produce palm oil here. Not only is vital forest, which is essential for our climate, destroyed, but also the habitat of many animals, for example many monkeys and apes such as orangutans. Palm oil is extracted from palm fruits.

For this reason, it is important to look for fair trade, sustainable cultivation and organic quality when buying! Palm fruits spoil quite quickly, so it is a good idea to buy them in frozen form.

Furthermore, special attention should be paid to the sufficient supply of essential minerals and a smooth digestion. Therefore, there are many breeders and keepers who offer their African Grey parrots cuttlebone, shell grit and/or a gritstone.

Cuttlebone is usually offered in powder form - or also as a "block" - and is a great mineral supplier because cuttlebone is particularly rich in calcium. Calcium is particularly important for bone health and also for egg production. Females and young animals in particular have an increased need for calcium. In the worst case, a deficiency can lead to severe bone disease, deformities, egg binding etc.

However, it is important to know that calcium can only be stored well in the bones if the body is sufficiently supplied with vitamin D3 (which is actually a hormone) and vitamin K2. Vitamin D3 and vitamin K2 play together here and work together. A sufficient supply of magnesium is also important in this context!

Therefore, cuttlebone is not only fed to birds, but also to reptiles. It is best to place a small bowl of cuttlebone powder in the aviary for the parrots to freely help themselves to.

Cuttlefish are squids. This is why cuttlefish powder smells strongly of fish. In addition to the important calcium, it also contains magnesium, zinc and iodine, for example.

If the birds do not like the smell of fish and sea, an odourless calcium powder can be used.

Calcium powders are divided into calcium citrate and calcium carbonate. Calcium citrate is artificially produced, while calcium carbonate is obtained from a naturally occurring source. Therefore, calcium carbonate usually has about four to five times the amount of calcium.

Whether African grey parrots need shell grit and/or a gritstone is quite controversial. Some keepers swear by this to aid digestion, others find it unnecessary and possibly even counterproductive.

A gritstone is supposed to provide birds with necessary minerals and stones for its gizzard. A gizzard is equipped with strong muscles. This type of stomach is a substitute for teeth, because in other animals - and of course also in humans - the comminution of food in the mouth takes place through the teeth (=chewing). In birds, the comminution of food takes place in the gizzard. To promote this comminution, a gritstone is often offered.

Nevertheless, it should not go unmentioned that some places also advise against the use of a gritstone. The reason for this is said to be that there were some specimens that took in too much grit and whose stomachs were too filled with stone chips. However, this rarely happens and is probably psychological. A healthy bird will only eat as much grit as it needs.

Grit stones are also said to be a burden on the digestion of birds that already suffer from digestive disorders because they are fed incorrectly by their owners. Of course, it must be said that grit does not cause healthy digestion but supports it. Healthy digestion must be achieved through a species-appropriate, varied and healthy diet - and grit then supports the comminution of this healthy food.

There are different types of grit. One type is shell grit. This is quite common and also quite popular with birds. Mussel grit consists of crushed mussel shells. It is extremely rich in calcium. However, mussel grit alone will not be able to cover the sufficient supply of calcium, because the bird simply does not need enough grit for this. The main function of grit is to break down the food in the stomach.

The subject of 'aspergillosis' should also be mentioned. Aspergillosis is a fungal disease in the lungs that has almost always been attributed to poor quality dry food. Low quality grain feed can sometimes be quite heavily contaminated with fungal spores, which is usually the case due to poor quality drying and poor storage. When feeding or breaking open these contaminated grains, the fungal spores can also get into the lungs and trigger a fungal disease there, which can spread from the lungs to other organs. Therefore, always make sure that the feed is of high quality.

© *Manfred Richter*

Suitable grains / seeds / legumes
(examples, not exhaustive)

Buckwheat

Peas (cooked, many proteins)

Barley

Oats

Hemp

Millet

Chickpeas (cooked, many proteins)

Kidney beans (cooked, lots of protein)

Pumpkin seeds (little, lots of fat)

Linseed

Lentils (cooked, lots of protein)

Maize corn

Milk thistle seeds

Pine nuts

Quinoa

Rapeseed

Rye

Turnipseed

Sesame

Sunflower seeds (little, high fat)

Wheat

Suitable vegetables (examples, not exhaustive)

Artichokes

Aubergines

Broccoli

Chicory

Endive lettuce

Lamb's lettuce

Fennel (good for soothing the digestion)

Cucumbers

Potatoes (well cooked)

Kohlrabi

Pumpkin

Sweet pepper

Radicchio lettuce

Romaine lettuce

Beetroot

Rucola

Celery

Spinach

Tomatoes (is strictly speaking a fruit)

Courgettes

Suitable fruits (examples, not exhaustive)

Apples

Pineapple

Bananas

Pears

Blackberries

Strawberries

Figs

Blueberries

Raspberries

Honeydew melon

Currants

Cherries

Kiwis

Passion fruit

Nectarines

Mangoes

Peaches

Papayas

Passion fruit

Watermelon

Grapes

<u>Suitable herbs (examples, not exhaustive)</u>

Sorrel

Common plantain

Nettle

Basil

Daisy

Camomile

Clover

Cress

Caraway

Dandelion

Lemon balm

Mint

Sage

Ribwort

Thyme

Chickweed

Suitable trees - branches and leaves (examples, not exhaustive)

Maple

Apple tree

Birch

Beech

Alder

Hazel

Pine

Cherry tree

Lime

Elm

Willow

Please do not feed under any circumstances!!

- Alcohol (hopefully no one will get this idea anyway)

- Avocado (parrots do not tolerate persine, can be fatal in the worst case)

- Coke and similar soft drinks

- Poisonous plants (e.g., yew, deadly nightshade, boxwood, meadow saffron, lily of the valley, etc. – some of them are deadly!)

- Cocoa / chocolate (parrots do not tolerate theobromine, can be fatal)

- Coffee

- Cabbage (many types of cabbage cause gassing; not always the case, but safety first)

- Nuts (lots of fat and risk of fungal spores - a shelled nut now and then as a treat is ok, but not necessary; domesticated parrots move much less than wild parrots and therefore have a lower calorie requirement)

- Salt

- Sweets and similar "human food" with a high sugar content like cakes etc.

© *Stefan Hallerbach*

Behaviour

The behaviours of birds in general and parrots in particular are sometimes very different from the behaviours of other animals or humans. Therefore, many gestures are often misinterpreted. The following is a brief overview of common parrot behaviours to avoid misinterpretation in the future and to interpret the behaviour correctly.

- Firmly pressing the plumage against the body:

When the African Grey Parrot clutches its feathers very tightly and sits motionless, it usually feels threatened and afraid of something or someone. It usually has its eyes wide open. This "stiffness" usually shows that the animal feels uncomfortable.

- Tapping a conspecific:

Sometimes a parrot will tap another bird in flight. Usually, this tapping is done with the feet and lasts only a short time. This is a dominance behaviour. The tapping parrot wants to show that it is the superior animal. This behaviour is no cause for concern. However, if the inferior bird is seriously attacked, possibly carried away and perhaps even bitten, this is obviously no longer a healthy behaviour.

- Sitting on one leg:

If the parrot is sitting on a perch or branch with one of its legs tucked up, this is perfectly normal. Parrots sometimes sit on one leg when they feel safe. Sometimes they sleep in this position. The plumage is usually a little fluffed up in this body position.

- Courtship:

Courtship means that one African Grey parrot courts another African Grey parrot because it wants to mate. The birds feed each other a lot and cuddle each other. Plumage is also often plucked and posed, and the birds often make "squeaking" sounds. The male will eventually try to climb onto the female's back to complete the mating. Even in couples that have been together for a long time, this behaviour still occurs frequently. In this way, the existing couple strengthens their relationship.

- Ducking and making small:

If a parrot does not want to argue with another parrot and/or wants to signal that it is subordinate to the other parrot, it often makes itself small and ducks down. Usually, it will tuck its feathers in tightly and lower its head as it does so.

- Egg laying:

Females lay eggs - whether or not these eggs have been fertilised by a mate. It is important that these eggs are not immediately taken away from the parrot, as this is not natural behaviour. If a female parrot lays eggs, she will want to hatch them. However, if humans take the eggs away from the bird, this can extremely stress the animal on the one hand. In addition, eggs are "reproduced" more quickly, which is of course very exhausting for the bird and deprives the body of more and more nutrients. If the eggs are fertilised by a partner, they should only be rendered infertile for a short time and then returned to the bird. For example, the eggs can first be frozen or shaken. The female will want to hatch the eggs, but if no young hatch - either because the eggs were not fertilised or were rendered infertile - she will leave the clutch herself. Then the eggs can be removed. The real eggs can also be replaced by dummies, which the female then tries to hatch. Whether the parrots notice this "fraud", however, is another question.

- Feather plucking:

If a parrot plucks out its feathers, this is usually due to a behavioural disorder. This behavioural disorder is most often triggered by loneliness.

- Lifting wings:

Sometimes African Grey parrots lift their wings very high, stretching them so high that they touch each other. This happens usually for two reasons: Either the animal just wants to stretch (the way we humans stretch our arms after waking up, for example), or it is to greet another African Grey parrot or to greet the human. However, if the wings are raised more to the side so that the parrot appears large, and if other threatening gestures are added, this is to impress other birds.

© Conger Design

- Regurgitating food:

Regurgitating up food should not be confused with vomiting. If a bird vomits, this is a symptom of disease, spoiled food or similar. In any case, the cause should be identified. However, deliberate regurgitation of food must be distinguished from this. The purpose of regurgitation is to feed another animal, usually a young animal. However, parrots sometimes also try to feed their partner, the person looking after them or even their mirror image. Mirrors can be very confusing to a parrot and if it tries to feed its own reflection, this is no longer normal behaviour. Also, if the parrot tries to feed the human, this can be a sign of loneliness. The human should not accept the food, of course.

- Yawning:

African grey parrots also yawn - just like we humans do. Yawning primarily serves to increase oxygen intake and is completely normal. However, above average yawning can be a sign of aspergillosis (see chapter "Diseases")! If a parrot yawns very often, it should be examined for this disease as a precaution.

- Head nodding:

Head nodding is perfectly normal and, in many cases, even occurs rhythmically. The parrot feels good and expresses joy by nodding its head. Many parrots even nod their heads rhythmically when they hear music they like. However, head nodding can also be used to attract attention.

- Growling:

Explaining growling is not necessary in principle - it means that the parrot is not feeling well and/or is threatening its counterpart.

- Scratching:

Parrots sometimes scratch themselves with their foot on different parts of their body. This is perfectly fine as long as it is not excessive. Humans also scratch themselves from time to time. However, if you notice that a parrot scratches itself very frequently, this can be a sign of a disease - for example, an infestation with mites or similar. In this case, the bird should be examined for parasites.

- Synchronised behaviour of two or more parrots:

When parrots exhibit the same behaviour, it is usually a sign that they get along very well and form a harmonious team. Parrots that feel they belong together often sleep together, fly around together, preen together, eat together, etc.

- Hanging overhead:

If a parrot lets itself hang with one leg or both legs from a branch, pole or rope, this is perfectly fine. This usually happens when the parrot is in a good mood and wants to play. It often makes shrill or squeaky sounds when it does this.

- Toe nibbling:

Nibbling on the toes with the beak is completely normal. This is the parrot's way of cleaning its feet and removing any debris. However, it can also be a sign that the parrot is embarrassed or does not know how to behave in a certain situation.

© *Wasi 1370*

Ten Common Diseases

Everyone gets sick sometimes. Some more often, others less often. Even birds such as African Grey parrots are not immune to diseases and the severity ranges from "very mild" to "potentially fatal". However, how often and how severely an African Grey parrot falls ill can be determined to a large extent.

As with humans, prevention is the be-all and end-all - an African Grey parrot that is kept in a species-appropriate manner, whose needs are met and which is fed a balanced and species-appropriate diet, is much less likely to fall ill than an African Grey parrot whose husbandry conditions are not optimal.

Of course, an animal can fall ill even if it is kept under perfect conditions, for example through heredity or sheer bad luck. However, many diseases can be prevented by taking precautions and will not occur if the owner knows about them and is prepared.

A species-appropriate and healthy diet should of course be the basis. It is also important to note that psychological problems such as stress or loneliness can also cause health problems.

It is not always necessary to visit the vet for every little thing. A visit to the vet is always stressful, because the African Grey parrot is torn away from its familiar environment and has to face a situation that is very stressful for it, which, including travel, can sometimes even take several hours.

Nevertheless, for liability reasons, I will not recommend self-treatment and self-medication. Especially beginners may misjudge diseases as they do not have much experience with African Grey Parrots.

I therefore point out that diseases must always be identified and professionally treated by a competent veterinarian.

When choosing a vet, make sure that the person chosen has experience with birds. This is an absolute must. Birds are so fundamentally different from other pets such as rodents, dogs, cats etc. that a bird cannot be treated by just any vet. A reputable vet will only treat an African Grey Parrot anyway if they feel confident to do so based on their experience and can treat the animal professionally.

In some areas it can be quite difficult to find a vet who knows birds well. This varies from region to region. It is possible that you may have to travel quite a long way to get there.

A long journey is of course more stressful for the animal, but it is better than having the animal treated by a vet who does not know birds well and may make mistakes. It is therefore a good idea to start looking for a suitable vet at an early stage so that the right person is immediately available in case of an emergency.

Of course, the owner must be sensitised to the recognition of diseases. If you know your animals, you will notice quite quickly if something is wrong and if an animal changes. Not every little change has to be a sign of a disease, but the following signs often indicate diseases - especially if they occur in a combination ...

... loss of appetite, refusal of food

... sudden aggressiveness and irritability

... unnatural movements

... changes in the shape, colour and/or consistency of the faeces

... loss of joy of movement

Although a disease is a case for the vet, the owner should be able to recognise the different diseases in principle. Therefore, we will now take a closer look at ten common and partly special parrot diseases.

1. Aspergillosis

In the chapter "Diet and Nutrition" we have already briefly mentioned aspergillosis. This disease is a fungal infection that mainly affects the lungs. The pathogens are tiny fungal spores of the genus "Aspergillus". These fungal spores are often inhaled when the animal eats, because they are often found in low-quality dried food or grain food that has not been properly dried and stored. This allows the fungal spores to accumulate and when the parrot eats the grains, the fungal spores also enter the lungs through the respiratory tract. From here, the infection can also spread quite quickly to other organs, such as the kidneys or liver. The reproductive organs such as the testicles or ovaries can also be affected by the infection, and this can lead to infertility.

If (initially) only the lungs are affected, it is called 'localised aspergillosis'. However, if the fungal infection has already spread to other organs, this is called 'diffuse aspergillosis'. Although poor quality food is often the trigger for aspergillosis, other triggers are also possible. The pathogens can also enter the parrot's body through the skin, for example through wounds or other injuries.

If the respiratory tract is infected first, the symptoms are similar to a cold - sneezing and similar symptoms often occur. In bad cases, the parrot has problems breathing and may even suffocate. So, this is a very serious disease. If the heart is affected, it can lead to cardiac arrest in the worst case. Therefore, the animal must be specifically examined for these fungal spores because a false diagnosis can have fatal consequences. The symptoms do not always appear immediately, and it can sometimes take a long time for the health condition to deteriorate.

In order to prevent an aspergillosis disease, it is of course important to provide high-quality food. Good storage should also be ensured. In any case, the feed should be stored in a cool and dry place, because moisture and heat can cause pathogens to form and spread very quickly. In addition, it is generally important to ensure good ventilation of the home as well as proper hygiene. Food remains and faeces should be removed regularly. Malnutrition can also favour an aspergillosis disease, because this naturally weakens the immune system. If the parrot is fed appropriately and provided with all important nutrients, the immune system can fight off pathogens much better.

The mental health of the bird should also be kept in mind, because a poor mental state also weakens the body and makes it more susceptible to disease. Loneliness, quarrels, too little space, too much noise or fear can be causes of poor mental health.

2. Avian Bornavirus and Proventricular Dilatation Disease

Avian Bornavirus and Proventricular Dilatation Disease ('PDD') go hand in hand, so we will look at them together. The avian bornavirus is the trigger for PDD.

Bornaviruses are the causative agents of Borna disease. This is a special animal disease (zoonosis) that tends to occur rather rarely in humans, but in the animal kingdom not only affects birds, but also, for example, sheep, horses, etc. Bornavirus is extremely dangerous for animals, as it can often cause fatal encephalitis.

It has now also been proven that Bornaviruses (more precisely: the avian Bornaviruses 'ABV') trigger PDD. This is a specific parrot disease that leads to the death of the animal. If a parrot has PDD, it is almost impossible to save it from death. It is therefore significant that avian bornaviruses have now been identified as the most likely trigger, because parrots can now be specifically tested for bornaviruses. PDD is very rare in other bird species, but quite common in parrots.

The typical symptoms are, for example, undigested grains in the animal's faeces, vomiting or weight loss, although the animal eats well. It is therefore important to pay attention to the digestion. If symptoms appear, the disease PDD has probably already broken out. Therefore, an early reaction should be taken if symptoms of avian bornavirus appear - in addition, for example, disorders of the locomotor system, balance disorders, plucking of feathers or trembling. In any case, the bird should be examined for bornaviruses in order to be able to treat it quickly and specifically in case of an infestation. Not every infestation with bornaviruses leads to PDD, but the risk must be minimised. Therefore, it is a good idea to have a parrot thoroughly checked for parasites as well as for typical viruses, such as the avian bornavirus, before taking it over.

3. Feather plucking

Feather plucking is a behavioural disorder that almost always has psychological causes. This behavioural disorder occurs very often in parrots, but less often in other birds. It is similar to the compulsive behaviour of humans, which is often also triggered by traumatic experiences or similar.

A parrot cleans and grooms its feathers. This is perfectly normal. However, if it suffers from psychological stress, it is quite likely that this plumage care will become a compulsive behaviour. The disorder becomes more and more intense and takes on abnormal proportions. The parrot not only preens itself, but literally plucks the feathers out of its skin. This becomes uncontrollable for a mentally ill parrot after some time. It of course causes massive damage to the plumage and the skin usually suffers as well. However, it only causes the parrot to want to "preen" itself even more intensively and the problem gets even worse. For example, plucking can also cause inflammation.

As already explained, the reasons for such a behavioural disorder are usually due to an unstable psyche. In very many cases, the affected parrot is simply very lonely - it has no partner or no friend. In this respect, parrots are quite similar to humans, because humans are also social animals and need social contacts. It is the same with the African Grey Parrot. Loneliness is very bad and stressful for him. When a parrot doesn't have a parrot friend, it will focus on the human. The human then needs to spend the majority of the time with the bird in order to prevent psychological problems. Other reasons can be, for example, lack of space, boredom, little variety, obesity, quarrels and fear.

But physical problems can also cause feather plucking. For example, malnutrition, hormonal disorders, infestation with fungi or parasites and the like. In any case, the cause of feather plucking must be investigated, because feather plucking itself is the symptom.

4. Egg binding

Egg binding is a very serious and urgent disease of a female African Grey Parrot. This disease not only affects birds such as parrots, but also other egg-laying animals, including reptiles, amphibians and fish. The causes can be manifold.

In principle, egg binding can have many different causes and can have different effects. In the worst case, however, it can also be fatal, which is why an avian veterinarian should always be consulted as soon as possible in the event of egg binding.

In egg binding, the eggs cannot be laid and are "stuck" in the body. This can usually be recognised by the fact that the bird's abdomen is swollen. Usually, the female tries to push the egg out by pressing hard, but in egg binding this is not possible. The condition also affects the digestive tract and often faeces are not passed as regularly as normal - this can also be a sign. Egg binding can also cause breathing problems and the bird may appear apathetic. Often the cloaca is bulging forward because the egg is supposed to come out but does not (possible prolapse). These symptoms should be given priority. Action must be taken quickly because this condition is very painful.

There are many causes of egg binding. Humans can prevent it, but there are also cases where egg binding has nothing to do with the husbandry conditions - for example, when the African Grey parrot is simply too young or too old to lay eggs.

Other common causes are, for example, permanent laying, malnutrition, primarily a lack of calcium, a lack of exercise opportunities, overfeeding (obesity), but also diseases of the laying gut (e.g., infections).

Calcium is not only an essential micronutrient for the bones, but also for the egg formation, because especially for the formation of the shell a lot of calcium is needed, which is withdrawn from the parrot's body. This is another reason why it is so important that the parrot always has enough calcium available.

In most cases, the skilled veterinarian can remove the egg without surgical intervention. Sometimes oxytocin is used for this. This is a hormone that stimulates egg laying. Vitamin supplements or a paraffin oil solution can also be helpful. Often the vet can use this to loosen the egg and massage it out. In some cases, for example if the egg is stuck, only surgery can help.

5. Mycoses and mycotoxicosis

We have already talked about the disease 'aspergillosis'. This disease and thus the genus of Aspergillus pathogens belong to the mycoses - mycoses are namely infections with a fungus in general. In addition, parrots can also be poisoned by the metabolic products of these fungi - this is called mycotoxicosis. Parrots are particularly susceptible to such diseases, which is why they are unfortunately also responsible for the premature death of many parrots.

The fungi that cause mycosis are not only Aspergillus, but also Mucor, for example. Mucor is a genus that belongs to the yoke fungi and are also widespread worldwide.

The greatest risk of mycosis is posed by low-quality feed if it has been dried and stored incorrectly. The fungi are not always visible! Therefore, it can also happen that already contaminated feed causes mycosis, even though the feed still appears fine on the outside. The causes and symptoms of any other mycosis are similar to those of aspergillosis, so the vet must examine the bird well and identify the pathogens in order to treat competently.

© *Conger Design*

6. PBFD (Psittacine Beak and Feather Disease)

PBFD is the abbreviation for "Psittacine Beak and Feather Disease". As the name suggests, this is a specific parrot disease ('psittacine').

Sometimes the disease is also abbreviated as BFDV (for 'Beak and Feather Disease Virus').

This disease must be taken extremely seriously as it is often fatal! It is also very contagious and can affect the partner animal or the rest of the flock within a short time.

This is a viral infection. The viruses belong to the so-called circoviruses, which are generally very contagious and difficult to eliminate. In fact, PBDF is the most common viral infection in parrots. Although it is rare in the wild, it is more common in domesticated parrots. In the wild, however, this viral disease also poses a great danger because it is so contagious - the animals usually live in larger flocks in the wild and therefore pass on the virus very quickly.

Before a new animal is acquired, it should always be thoroughly examined - also for PBFD, because the incubation period for these viruses is very long. This means that a parrot can carry the virus for months before it shows the first symptoms. Therefore, prevention is the be-all and end-all!

Symptoms include poor plumage condition (severe thinning) or malformation of the beak. Of course, it should not come to that in the first place, so it is advisable to have the viruses diagnosed by the vet at an early stage so that treatment can take place in time.

7. Polyomaviruses

Polyomaviruses occur in both birds and other vertebrates and can also be transmitted to humans. They cause infections and the viruses can even remain in the body after an infection has been overcome. This is called "pathogen persistence". The viruses nest in different parts of the body of the respective host and survive even the healing of the infection.

An infection with polyomaviruses can be very severe or very mild in birds. If the immune system is good, an infection may not even be noticed. However, in the worst case scenario, polyomaviruses can also lead to the death of the animal, although this is rather rare in African Grey Parrots. More susceptible to polyomaviruses are, for example, budgerigars (which also belong to the family of 'true parrots' / Psittacidae), because unfortunately the infection is often fatal in them.

Healthy African grey parrots, on the other hand, usually have a mild course. Nevertheless, an infection should of course be avoided, and it is best not to keep African Grey parrots together with budgies.

The virus is usually transmitted via cells of the feathers and the skin as well as via the faeces.

8. Psittacine herpes virus (Pacheco's disease)

Psittacines Herpesvirus (= Pacheco's Disease) is also a viral infection, but it is a herpes virus. It is a very serious disease because it is often fatal and because the condition of the sick animal usually deteriorates extremely quickly. This virus has a very short incubation period of about five days to one week and therefore breaks out very quickly. In the case of this virus infection, quick action is imperative, because the death rate is well over 50% (more like two-thirds).

The virus is transmitted from host to host via bodily excretions; mostly via faeces. In the environment, it cannot survive for long without a host, whereas it is very survivable in a host body. Often it is not even noticed that the virus is in the respective body - until it finally breaks out. This usually happens due to extreme stress, as with other herpes viruses.

African grey parrots are not among the most endangered species that are very sensitive to this virus, but even with them the disease may be fatal. The tricky thing is that once the disease has broken out, the animal's condition often deteriorates very quickly. Symptoms range from diarrhoea and blood in the faeces to breathing difficulties and vomiting. However, not all symptoms need to be present - for example, severe diarrhoea may remain the only symptom. Nevertheless, the disease must always be identified by the veterinarian and treated professionally - and quickly, because the animal's condition can deteriorate seriously very quickly.

9. Psittacosis (avian chlamydiosis)

Psittacosis is also called 'avian chlamydiosis'. It is not a virus, but a bacterial infectious disease that mainly affects parrots, but can also spread to humans and other animals. Similar to the previously presented virus, the Chlamydophila psittaci bacterium is also transmitted via body excretions (faeces, secretions, etc.). An important difference, however, is that this bacterium can survive for a very long time without a host.

Whether the disease breaks out depends, as is often the case, on how well the parrot can defend itself against the bacteria. Older parrots, stressed parrots or parrots that are malnourished naturally have a poorer immune system and cannot fight off bacteria and viruses as well as happy and healthy parrots that are supplied with all essential nutrients.

If the disease breaks out, the symptoms include, for example, problems with breathing, rapid weight loss, apathetic behaviour, sometimes conjunctivitis, diarrhoea with simultaneous loss of appetite, blood in the faeces and/or even convulsive tremors. These same symptoms, as I'm sure you've noticed, can also be found in some other diseases. This is why it is so important that the expert veterinarian clearly identifies the disease in order to be able to treat it in a targeted manner. Psittacosis can be treated very successfully with antibiotics in most cases.

10. Worms

Worms belong to the group of parasites. Parasites are divided into 'endoparasites' and 'ectoparasites'.

Ectoparasites are 'external-living' parasites, for example mites on the skin. Endoparasites are 'inside-living' parasites.

Worms are therefore classified as endoparasites. They include tapeworms (cestodes), hairworms (capillaria), roundworms (ascarids) and the like.

Almost all animals are infested by parasites sooner or later and this is usually easily treatable. However, in artificially created habitats - for example, in aviaries - an infestation increases quite quickly if it is not recognised and treated at an early stage, because there is not too much space available in the cage.

How strong or weak the parasite infestation is often also strongly depends on the animal's psyche. Stress, fear, loneliness and other negative feelings weaken the animal's immune system and thus its defences. If an animal is infested with worms, this can usually be recognised quite easily from the faeces. The consistency of the faeces usually becomes soft and resembles mush, and in acute infestation there is often severe diarrhoea.

Sometimes worms can even be seen on the faeces; however, this is not always the case and depends on what kind of worm the parrot is infested with. In addition, the sick animal often loses weight (sometimes rapidly), even with a good diet. In particularly severe cases, intestinal rupture or intestinal obstruction can occur. It is best to have the animal examined about once a year as a preventive measure or at least to send faecal samples to a laboratory every year (or every six months).

© *Capri 23*

Legal Notice

This book is protected by copyright. Reproduction by third parties is prohibited. Use or distribution by unauthorised third parties in any printed, audio-visual, audio or other media is prohibited. All rights remain solely with the author.

Author: Alina Daria Djavidrad

Contact: Wahlerstraße 1, 40472 Düsseldorf, Germany

© 2021 Alina Daria Djavidrad

1st edition (2021)

© Wasi 1370

© *Karolyn*

Room for Notes

Printed in Great Britain
by Amazon

17221236R00066